Building People Building Kingdoms

Book One:

The Business Plan

By: Lia Abney

Foreword by: Dr. Yvonne Jackson

Book Cover Photo Credit:

Bobby Hill, One Love Photography

Copyright © 2018 LIA ABNEY

ALL RIGHTS RESERVED

No parts of this book may be distributed or transmitted in any form by any means, graphics, electronics, or mechanical, including photocopy, recording, taping, or by any information storage or retrieval system, without permission in writing from the author, except in the case of reprints in the context of reviews, quotes, or references.

DEDICATION

First and foremost giving God all the glory for trusting me with the vision. Father, you could have chosen another, so I thank you. To my children (DeJuan, Tyler, and Chontele) you are worth all the sacrifice and I hope you all are proud of me as I am proud of each of you – this is for you – it's all about *legacy building*. To Mother Smith love you for all you are not just to your family but to those whom you have spiritually adopted as your own.

The Business Plan

The Business Plan

Table of Contents

DEDICATION 3

ACKNOWLEDGEMENT 7

FOREWORD 9

INTRODUCTION 13

Chapter 1 – Legacy 17

Chapter 2 – Identity 21

Chapter 3 – Courage 27

Chapter 4 – Inspiration 32

Chapter 5 – Accountability 36

Chapter 6 – Mentor 40

Chapter 7 – The Business Plan 49

   Business Startup Checklist 55

Chapter 8 – The Boardroom 57

Glossary 62

About the Author 64

The Business Plan

ACKNOWLEDGEMENT

To my girl Lisa, thanks for the inspiration and to encourage me to let my voice be heard. To Bobby Hill (One Love Photography) for capturing the vision through your talents as a photographer – both of your support is most appreciated.

Foreword Credit: To Dr. Yvonne Jackson thank you for being my original supporter (spiritually and professionally). You saw beyond this hot mess. You also saw beyond the vision and was willing to walk this out with me through the process, the tears, and some confusing times. *Building People – Building Kingdoms* the series is here! God's plan...Yay!!

Editing credit: Gosh...I don't even know where to begin. Prophetess Rosetta Parker-Austin (founder/owner of Watchman Warriors Foundation). You saw me and you let me be me. The first eyes to see the book in raw form and you readily and you were willing to put the finishing touch on God's work. Through tears...I humbly thank you. Agape.

The Business Plan

The Business Plan

FOREWORD

It's not strange to feel like you were born with a special meaning, or with a thought that you were put here for a particular reason. Perhaps you were put here to help another person in some special way or you have a brilliant idea of how to make millions but don't know where to start. It is part of human nature to desire meaning and purpose, yet we often find ourselves struggling with day to day challenges of how to fulfill our purpose or even know what our purpose really might be. Perhaps some of us want to own a business, or be a successful professional with a lot of money, it really doesn't matter if you do or don't. Yet we must not forget that the Lord our God has given each of us the ability to produce wealth (Deuteronomy 8:18). As you will learn through the materials presented in the Building People – Building Kingdoms Series *The Business Plan - a Legacy Journey*, wealth is not always defined monetarily.

The Business Plan

As you are seeking direction with your God given ability, there is a mindset one must develop but you cannot be reluctant to embrace the unknown. The information that is disseminated in your "Legacy Journey" is paramount for the believer's day to day walk, and it will serve as a vital tool in being conditioned to break the bondage of fear and the lack of self-confidence. By doing so will allow you to discover the vast opportunities that awaits you in ways you never knew existed.

As you take hold of the concepts outlined in the chapters, you will come to understand the true meaning of endurance, something I like to call "stick-to-it-ness". You will be able to gain more self-assurance in your abilities, and be encouraged to pursue your destiny full steam ahead, with a "don't quit, don't give up" attitude. I am particularly appreciative of Ms. Abney's tenacity, keen insight into the business world, coupled with humility, love and her expressed desire to see the people of God become fully equipped. Through the Building People – Building Kingdoms series she provides the necessary tools and motivation that will propel you forward as you embrace your "Legacy Journey".

Safe travels and God Speed,

Dr. Yvonne Jackson

The Business Plan

Page intentionally left blank.

INTRODUCTION

For I know the plans I have for you, declares the LORD, plans for wholeness and not for evil, to give you a future and a hope.

The Scripture above Jeremiah 29:11 (ESV), has been the driving force to achieve all that God has planned for me. Unfortunately, I didn't have anyone to guide me about how to get there. It meant I had to get beyond my own fears of inadequacy and failures. I had to open myself up and allow others to enter my life. I did not understand that it was okay to have a small circle of those that I could trust rather than none at all.

Some of my internal thoughts were: *I accomplished much with little satisfaction still feeling empty. Yes, I completed many things in my life but achieved nothing. The main journey was allowing myself room to fail without shame –* **I am just not feeling this (screaming in my head)***. Allowing the holes in my life to be filled with the best God had to offer for me –* **Lord, can't I just mind my own business.** *To realize that my troubles, my negative thoughts about myself,*

The Business Plan

and coping mechanisms where barriers to pursuing God's best for me and building a life that brought me peace, love, and joy – **okay, God I surrender***...I'm not sure what I am really getting myself into...but okay.*

It wasn't long until I really accepted (through many tears) I belonged in this world (that I have a purpose) to make a difference not *just* too merely exist. But there are times when I would allow my emotions to get in the way or *I* would just get in the way. See, I would begin building but I was not willing to take it to the next level. Although I was aware of what was required, I was not trusting of others to help me. Rest assured, I have by no means have arrived but I cannot and will not stop. Because I am not my own. Nor do I have to be alone in this journey.

I have to say, my fear was not based on *if* I could do it rather it was *how* would I do it. And believe it or not I was not even worried about the money. As I have heard from many Elders in the church and I so believe this today — it's God's vision, so it's His provision. Sounds crazy...I know. As I accepted this journey many would come to me inquiring about how to start a business or how to overcome barriers in their lives. Then it happened…my purpose…*Building People – Building Kingdoms*…of course it required for me to share with someone who coined this as a motto for the vision that God had given me – thank you Dr. Yvonne Jackson. It became very clear and I accepted the plans God had for me. This doesn't mean I don't wonder off course from time to time either. But deep down inside I also know that I can't leave this world without sharing what has been deposited in me with others therefore worrying about the *how* would only become my excuse of why I am not doing it. Well, I don't know about you. But I'm curious to see what this journey is all about through my failures and successes.

So, the legacy journey begins…

This is intended to be a series of interactive books to motivate and encourage you. I love words. Words are powerful. Knowing the true meaning and origin of a word can change how you view the world around you. And you will be more careful about what you speak concerning your life and those whom you care about. This is why I have included a glossary of terms throughout this book. Although the feel of this book is based on an entrepreneur's point of view anyone that desires can apply the practical principles economically, socially, and spiritually in their lives. May your legacy journey take you to another level of believing in yourself and move you beyond emotional and physical barriers to draw you closer to achieving your dream.

I hope you are ready because it's time to BUILD PEOPLE – BUILDING KINGDOMS.

Lia Abney

Chapter 1 – Legacy

"You must decide if you are going to rob the world or bless it with the rich, valuable, potent, untapped resources locked away within you."

- Dr. Myles Munroe, *Understanding your Potential, Discovering the Hidden You*

Legacy is a result of where your experiences produce outcomes handed down from the past to the next generation (Proverbs 13:22). For legacy to manifest in your life it requires **resiliency**, determination, and fortitude; to overcome the bad times and to rise above the challenges and obstacles of life. However, there is something you need to know. Legacy is not always **tangible** nor monetary (with a lot of zeros behind that dollar sign).

We like to limit legacy to property or a title but I want to tell you that is not always the

The Business Plan

case. Perhaps you don't desire to own a business or don't have an inheritance to pass on. Legacy can be defined as a mindset that causes changes to the way we think or a behavior passed on from one generation to another. This change of mindset can manifest in a myriad of prosperity in various areas of your life.

Maybe you would like to work a company or within a certain profession based on your purpose. Well, that's okay. But how are you going to get there? What would you like to leave behind? Are you going to do it by yourself? Or are you willing to change? Or you even willing to ask for help?

The journey towards building requires you to have all the necessary resources (i.e. materials, funds, and a strong foundation). You and I both have heard the many stories of those in the teaching profession that have impact a former student so much that it changed the course of their lives. Well, that level of impact in itself, is a legacy. Why? Because that same caring nature, that same attitude of serving others and sharing of resources…that same courage will be passed on to others in the same manner it was received. You got it – LEGACY.

A legacy mindset can affect any area in your life if you apply it. However, holding onto an old mindset will take you absolutely nowhere. This level of change requires a constant discovery of opportunities and ideas that impacts and changes the course of your journey in building a legacy. In other words, get rid of old thoughts and implant a new way of thinking about your future.

In the next chapters, I want to share with you 4 key components that will guide you on your legacy journey. Also, additional chapters will focus on the benefits of having a mentor as well as key components for developing a business plan and importance of having a board of directors.

The Business Plan

Chapter 2 – Identity

Identity – connect with who you are and what you or your organization represents.

I strongly believe that our words create how we see ourselves – your identity. First, I am a woman of faith and the Bible shows from Genesis to Revolutions how our words can change things. Don't believe me? Well, God spoke and created the heavens and the earth and everything in it – and it manifested. If my God created me in His image and gave me dominion over EVERYTHING then I have that same power on the inside of me to speak. Thus, I can speak to myself to create a positive mindset that moves me in my purpose and so do you.

So, if I was to ask you to tell me who you are (your identity) using just three words.

The Business Plan

What would you say? Well, let's take a moment to do just that. Now, I want you to look in the mirror and read aloud the words you have written below. Why, because I believe our words creates and changes what we have been telling ourselves; as well as what others have spoken over us. It wipes out negative words that has been planted in our subconscious thinking that has shaped how we see ourselves in the here and now which can affect our decisions for the future. So, let's get started. Go ahead I'll wait…:

I AM…*now jot down three words below.*

1. _____
2. _____
3. _____

So, are you done? Awesome. The exercise you completed above will help you to identify character traits that will shape your ideal life and how you see yourself. The words you speak daily can set your mind and attitude in the right direction towards building a legacy. Let me repeat this. As you grow through life's cycle these words can change. I believe in keeping it simple. If three is not enough – write down a few more. This is a daily task and a process. It will not happen overnight.

Let's look at this in a natural way. So, for instance, if one of your words is "creative" you might find that you are the artsy type or quite the entertainer. Or perhaps you are a deep thinker – analytical. This could lead to exploring activities and opportunities that bring you great joy as well as connect you with others that will positively influence the direction you are going. So let's take this a little further.

I love art. As a little girl, I enjoyed painting by the numbers especially horses. Although I have not painted in quite a while. Now, I have rediscovered the interest and so I now have ventured to exploring and participating in activities that centers on art such as, sip

The Business Plan

and paint or local fundraising events that feature local artists. As I enjoy these events in support of others, I use these opportunities to network and meet others who may know other people willing to support my vision. Also, these encounters have developed into friendships that I previously did not have. See how that works?

I know this seems simple for some. However have you ever met someone that found it hard to get out and explore places alone or with people they didn't know? Well, if you feel your purpose is ministry or an entrepreneur interacting with others in a social setting can be challenging. So, how do you get beyond feeling socially awkward? Using this practical step of using words to identify positive attributes about myself has changed how I think and feel about my role in those type settings.

It's very challenging for me to interact in a social setting so as I speak words such as "*I'm an inspiration to others.*" Yet that is not going to happen unless I believe it, receive it, and act on it (now that sounds like faith to me). In order to be an inspiration to others, it requires me to interact with others. So, I challenge myself by finding unique things that I enjoy and use these opportunities to grow. This world is so full of technology that the skill of social engagement is becoming a lost art. It's so easy to hide behind a keyboard and spew my beliefs and ideas but can I engage another to encourage them and just give a little bit of myself to help a sister or brother out.

And, I also found through this process, that I had an inner desire to share knowledge. I wasn't sure to whom or how but by identifying WHO I AM. Well, this led me to discover that I truly had a desire to write which has also manifested into a nonprofit organization to help others achieve their goals in life.

The Business Plan

So, what is on the inside of you? What are you supposed to plant in the earth but *you* keep blocking *yourself or allowing others to define who you are*? It's time to shed your old thinking and make that move!

Chapter 3 – Courage

Courage – do what it takes; don't quit; be willing to put it all on the line.

Courage requires you to actively pursue your destiny even when things are challenging you from all sides. There is one thing I want you to clearly understand – the trials and struggles you go through are only designed to shape you but they do not define who you are. Although I might be a divorcee it's not who I am – let's clarify this. I am not a woman scorned nor is there anything wrong with me (no I'm not perfect). As a matter of fact, I pray and speak blessings over my children's father and his new family rather than to speak harmful words over their lives. It does me absolutely no good to dwell on the past. Doing so can affect my thinking about how could I see myself as a victim rather than an overcomer. The point is, if you and I hold on to the hurt next thing you know we may resort to speaking mean and hateful words. Maybe

The Business Plan

not to others – but in our mind which would be a terrible waste not to mention toxic to our purpose. *And, for what?*

Look, I am still believing in my future husband to come a knocking at my door, yes Lord (*giggling on the inside*). This journey requires us to put everything on the line – feelings, doubts, and name – it takes *courage*. Yes, even our name. Perhaps like you, I didn't want everyone knowing who I am; exposing myself. Really? Knowing our private business and inconsistencies. Shucks.

My Thoughts: I do not proclaim to have super powers (nope no capes here) *nor do I just want to jump...my process is a little complicated lol. However, I wouldn't have it any other way. Why? Because it's for me. Just like your process and what you have to endure is for you. You just need to have the courage to prevail and travel that road constructed just for you.*

The Business Plan

To have courage requires you to take a risk. Building a legacy requires risk. This is where you, will need to expose a little of yourself each day in this journey. Every time you expose an area, you shed a little of your old self. But I promise you it is for your good. The new you shines through and shows up.

I would have rather been in my home minding my own business rather than exposing myself to the world (*like really – eyes rolling and giggling*). But I have to tell you - eye have not seen nor have ear heard what God has prepared (1Cor 2:9) for you. So, you and I cannot worry about what others think or what they might say. No, it's time to stop hiding. I have a greater purpose and so do you. This journey requires you to be courageous but is not for the weak and faint of heart. If you don't walk it out, who will hear and who will see the works of the Lord with you?

When I graduated from high school before going into the military, I was told that I would not make it. Here I was leaving home at 18 years old and this is what resonated within me. Scared and alone going off to who knows where. Of course, I was stubborn and was determined to make it no matter what but those words still haunted me for *years. As a result,* it determined the course of my decisions and even looking for love in all the wrong places (ugh). Until I started speaking something different to myself every day. Words that I am still speaking today.

Those words are…

John 3:16 - *For God so loved the world that he gave his one and only Son, that whoever believes in him shall not perish but have eternal life.*

Deuteronomy 31:6 – *Be strong and courage. Do not be afraid or terrified because of them, for the Lord your God goes with you; he will never leave you nor forsake you.*

These biblical words changed how I saw myself, how not to feel lonely or afraid in this journey. These faith building words will continue to help you and I to fully accept that we are worthy of God's love and promises despite our shortcomings. Those words became a source of strength when I was going through my divorce, ministry, relationship, financial and job challenges. It taught me how to be courageous. That I had someone greater on my side on this journey. I couldn't see the plan but I began to know that it exists. I now just needed to pursue it and trust it.

Perhaps your source of strength is obtained through other means. Whatever it is accept it and use it to the fullest to get the most out of your hopes and dreams. No matter what, don't settle for less. Do not allow trouble to trouble you. And absolutely do not make excuses (period).

The Business Plan

Chapter 4 – Inspiration

Inspiration – not for self-interest but to serve others.

I AM an inspiration and inspired to guide others. I have this as one of my motivational phrases taped to my monitor at work. It is a constant reminder for me to treat others that are difficult and hard to work with – with kindness, patience, and understanding (I'm a work in progress - lol). This does not mean either of us should be a pushover it merely means to use wisdom in our decisions, spoken words, and not to consider ourselves to be above others. The manner in which you treat others is how you want to be treated – yes, the golden rule. It is also a reminder not to be difficult as well.

A simple principle but it is often forgotten when we get into the business mindset or ministry. Or even when you are faced with difficult times. Remember the definition for legacy is something passed on to others not just something for our own selfish needs or gratification. So, ask yourself the following questions below:

1. Why am I doing what I am doing?

_____

_____

_____

_____

2. Who will it impact?

_____

_____

_____

_____

The Business Plan

3. What will others gain?

_____

_____

_____

_____

4. Am I making a sacrifice to help others?

_____

_____

_____

_____

The purpose of this is to get all of the emotional reasons and excuses out of the way. Focusing more on who it will impact will make you less likely to make it all about you. A legacy journey is not solely focused on you. Remember it is about the lives you want to impact.

The Business Plan

Now if you did not respond to the questions on the previous pages. I encourage you to go back and reflect and write your responses down. Believe it or not during this process, you have actually begun to develop your business plan.

Chapter 5 – Accountability

Accountability – opportunity and responsibility to uphold the legacy to strengthen your family and your business.

Dr. Myles Monroe is a person I have admired for his leadership and business acumen. He was also a great inspirational leader who shared his knowledge with countless others. I would venture to say the success that he left behind is legacy for his family and many other generations which would not have been possible without accountability.

Being accountable to someone else is a scary thought on its own. Those that have made a conscious decision to not pursue their purpose might very well be because of fear of accountability and exposure in their journey. Your journey might have a lot of twists and turns. Not to mention a few valleys and hills which might expose some areas or unfamiliar environments in your life. Some of this will result in revealing mess that you have covered up overtime.

I don't know about you but even when we were birthed into this world none of us emerged from the womb squeaky clean. The nurses and doctors had some serious cleaning to do. Even when a new mother receives their new bundle of joy there is still some of the after-birth residue in the creases of that soft, new baby skin. Yet the look on the parent's face indicates the nine-month journey was more than worth it.

When we think about it the same thing occurs regarding the time spent with our purpose or with a plan during our own legacy journey. We are not going to have everything perfect. We will be exposed and in most cases, find we have a little residue left over from our failures. The great thing is that we are not required to be perfect in this journey to legacy. Waiting for perfection delays the process and growth; not to mention that you will miss opportunities for something great to manifest in your life or to be a blessing to others.

Likewise, we are now accountable to others just like the new parents with their new born child. Being accountable just makes it easier for you to get through areas with the possibility of just having a little residue. Accountability can be fostered through relationships with other leaders or even through a board that is established to guide you through your decisions.

The Business Plan

So, let's do a short review. There are 4 principles in Chapters 2- 5. List them below:

1._____

2._____

3._____

4._____

Chapter 6 – Mentor

Mentor – an experienced, trusted advisor.

One thing that I also consider of value in building a legacy is the benefit of having a mentor. Over my 30 years in corporate America has consistently revealed most individuals stating that having a mentor during their journey has helped them to make sound decisions and greatly impact their career progression in a positive way. And guess what? You don't have to just limit yourself to just one mentor– it is not a competition. It's about growth. A mentor is there without judgement during the hard times, your failures, and successes to encourage you. Having a mentor or someone you can trust to push you beyond yourself is priceless in your legacy journey.

Growing up without a mother, I have learned to value the women in my life who have helped to navigate difficult times and stuck places. However, it has not always been that way. Because of the hurt I have experienced from people (*period*). I often find it difficult to connect with others on a personal level. Well, a woman, that I affectionately call Mother Smith is one whom I can call on when I just want to say, "Hi, how was your day? I just wanted to let you know that I was thinking about you and that I love you."

If I am to be honest there was this empty place in me that causes me to lose hope sometimes to withdraw from the world around me and disconnect more often than not. Can you imagine if Rosa Parks had hidden from the world? How about Susan B. Anthony? Would woman have the rights they have today? But because I was willing to open myself up to connect with others despite an absent mother I am now pursing my purpose. It doesn't take people you know biologically to encourage you, to push you to greatness. It simply takes a well written out plan and to be connected to others. You see Mother Smith is my mentor

The Business Plan

– she is my spiritual mother. I love her dearly and I thank God for her.

And there is Lisa. God placed her in my life at the time I needed her the most. I'm so thankful for my girl Lisa. She is not perfect and she might not even know it but she is my mentor, my confident, and my mental check. She has helped me to discover things about myself I didn't know. Help me to see that I am courageous when I feel defeated and helpless. The days I wanted to give up, the days I just…wanted to…*give…up*. She reminds me so often that I am needed. What is on the inside of me is valuable. She reminds me I have a purpose and she watches out for me.

See a mentor is not just one that is absent and sometimes available when the mood strikes them. They are *there*. So, I value her boldness her go get it attitude which has become a model for me to emulate. She doesn't advise me on what to do, she tells me how to do it. And it doesn't cost me a thing – just my time and effort. God is so mindful to place precious jewels in our lives while on this journey to building a legacy.

Now, some of you could say *"...not me, I don't need anyone telling me what to do, not today. I'm my own "Boss"*.

Well, Okay.

Eventaully like me, you will have to arrive at a point where you will say "yes." On one particular day, the things she told me to do were the things I needed to do. In frustration admittedly, I told her in so many words verbally and nonverbally what I was and was NOT going to do (with an ugly expression on my face).

Ultimately, because God cares for you and I He will send someone who can could get through to us. For me, that individual helped me me to think differently which impacted my decisions. Of course, once I calmed down and left Madness Avenue I'm back on track pursuing destiny.

The Business Plan

As a matter of fact, Lisa is the reason why I am writing to you today. With an urgency in her voice – *"why are you not speaking to women – you need to be heard"*. This is not to leave our strong men out of the process or to think of ourselves independent from them – we need them too but this is to encourage my sisters – *all sisters*.

So here I am. Think how wonderful it will be to tell your children or grandchildren that the legacy you are building for them was built with a determination to forge a path of greatness for them and the next generation.

Having a mentor can encourage you and push you beyond yourself (fears, doubts and yes, your haters) it is something that is essential to accomplishing our goals our dreams - everything. I am talking about LEGACY.

We all need someone who will say,
-You need to stop trippin' -Really? No one can do what you do! You're fabulous and made for this!

The Business Plan

-Go BE THE CEO YOU ARE MEANT TO BE!
-Follow the plan.
~All I can say is "thanks Lisa".

While we may not get it right every day, we cannot refuse to leave this earth without emptying everything God has put on the inside of us. At least by doing our very best. So, I encourage you to connect with someone, In fact, it does not need to be someone that is in the same industry as yourself – all it requires is mutual respect and genuine engagement from both parties.

How do I know this? For example, remember my girl Lisa. By profession she is in IT and I am a Management Analyst, however we both have a friendship where our passion for our community interconnects. We don't always think alike, we don't necessarily like the same things, nor do the same things, or even have the same fashion sense (smiling)! I love my chucks (known as Converse athletic shoes) (laughing out loud). But the connection is a divine one where God placed us in each other's lives to encourage, to build and to push each other to soar like eagles (Isaiah 40:31).

Perhaps you have a mentor and really haven't engaged them in a while, I encourage you to reach out to them. Sometimes life gets in the way, however cultivating relationships first begins with a willingness to be an active participant and requires work by all parties.

We should all be challenged to learn from the lessons that will mold us into the kind of leader and business professional for our next generation – as well as for yourself.

Mentors are also great resources to connect you with potential supporters, sponsors, or advisors as business owner.

Just a small note – mentoring relationships requires give and take. Don't take for granted those that share themselves in your journey. Be kind and supportive to them…

The Business Plan

Sharing an internal thought: *"This is not an individual journey this is a legacy journey. A legacy for your family for generations to come. Be the butterfly in your family. Come out of your cocoon and pollinate the world with your greatness, your beauty and brilliancy and color the world with your innovative ideas for a greater tomorrow. This is your LEGACY!"*

So, here is a short exercise. Write below the names of at least two individuals (current or someone you admire) to be your mentor. After writing them below, take the time on this week to reach out to them and schedule a meeting rather it be virtual or in person (of course I encourage a face-to-face meeting). Then if agreed upon, you can schedule regular meetings that best fits both schedules.

List of potential mentors (at least two):

1. _____

Phone:_____

Email:_____

The Business Plan

Next Meeting:_____

2. _____

Phone:_____

Email:_____

Next Meeting:_____

The next two chapters are bonuses for those who may desire to start a new business. However, I encourage to find out more about the local resources that are available to help you in your legacy journey.

Chapter 7 – The Business Plan

DEFINITION: *A business plan is a roadmap to guide you on how the organization is structured and managed. The plan also considers future growth opportunities. This plan gives a visual guide for investing and to gain buy-in from potential investors.*

Believe it or not everything we have just covered is the beginning of a business plan. Identifying areas that makes you different; asking questions about what you have to offer ,and knowing what makes you tick (or risks you are willing to take). You discovered the things that will make you push beyond you; explore new areas of interest for creative and innovative ideas; and build and connect new relationships. All of these are just steps towards building a business and personal growth.

The take away from this chapter is to have a plan. There is no specific format in which one is to be completed. But you are encouraged to have one. In addition, this is a working document. *Always, (I repeat) Always* review your plan – quarterly or annually include a review process in your objectives.

Two Types of Plans:

1. A Traditional Plan Includes:
- **Executive Summary** – include mission statement, product or service, basic information (i.e. location, number of employees, **high-level growth** plan).
- **Company Description** – detailed information on problems you solve as well as business and customers you plan to serve. *Here is where you outline your organization's strengths.*
- **Market Analysis** – market outlook.
- **Organization and Management** – legal structure of the organization (i.e. LLC). As well as chart to identify levels of leadership or departments.
- **Marketing and Sales Strategy** – how do you plan to attract your customers and clients.

- o **Funding Requirements** – outline your funding requirements.
- o **Financial Projections** – provide a 5-year forecast of expenditure budgets, cash flow, income statements, collateral, balance sheets that match your funding requests.
- o **Appendix** – supporting documents (i.e. licenses, resumes, credit histories, permits, legal documents, or contracts) if applicable.

- **A Lean Start Plan Includes**:
  - o **Key Partnerships** – other collaboration opportunities or community based partnerships with other agencies (i.e. suppliers, manufacturers, subcontractors, or strategic partners).
  - o **Key Activities** – what are the organizations goals to gain the advantage? Such as technology, marketing, direct or indirect sales.
  - o **Key Resources** – list resources of most important assets (staff, property, capital).

The Business Plan

- **Value Statement** – a statement on the unique value the organization brings to the community.
- **Customer Relationships** – customer engagement (i.e. face to face or online) services.
- **Customer Segments** – specifics on target audience.
- **Cost Analysis** – define strategy for addressing funding opportunities (reducing cost or maximizing value).
- **Communication Strategy** – how the organization communicates with its customers.
- **Cash Flow** – how will the organization make money.

Sharing an external thought: *"I'm going to encourage you not to get overwhelmed by the process. It is necessary to achieve your dreams and to build an empire for your children. This process is yours and yours alone. Take it easy on yourself – this means take care of you first. Have the right people around you to encourage you – this means to remove unnecessary negative talk, people, and distractions that will get you off course. Shut it all down!*

The Business Plan

Thinking through the process of developing a business plan requires patience and the ability to persevere through the low moments. Having people to support you in the process can be important and can be a game changer for your reaching and achieving your goals. An ability to assess your environment (internal and external) to identify resources to meet your goals as well can alleviate the drain on your strength to just keep moving.

There are many ways to assess your resources using different methods of analysis such as **SWOT analysis** or a **gap analysis** just to mention a few.

It's okay to take a break in the developmental phases. However, set goals that will help you to stay consistent and motivated. Use your support system to reach out to get a pulse check (reality check). Then keep it moving.

The Business Plan

On the next page, you will notice that I have enclosed a checklist to help you with the development of your business plan.

Business Startup Checklist

DATE COMPLETED	ACTION
	Market Research
	Write your business plan
	Fund your business
	Pick your business location
	Choose type of business (i.e. LLC, nonprofit…)
	Choose your business name
	Register your business
	Get federal and state tax IDs (an EIN)
	Apply for licenses and/or zoning permits
	Open a business bank account

The Business Plan

For more information on small business startups visit the Small Business Administration website at *https://www.sba.gov/business-guide/plan/write-your-business-plan-template#section-header-2*

Another great source is your local chamber or business league associations.

Chapter 8 – The Boardroom

You might be saying why do I need all these people when I can do it myself? *"You can, but I am here to tell you that if you are anything like me and the vision given to you is greater than yourself. Accountability is your best friend and a blessing. I don't want you to get burnt out before you even begin. There are so many people that needs what is on the inside of you – I might need it. This is the time to release it into the world and the easiest way to burnout is to think you are the only one that can make it happen. Yes, you have been given the vision but it is not yours to bare alone. There are others that have been purposed to help and support you. Now it requires faith and trust to reach out and let others be great too."*

Don't worry if you don't have a board right away. I didn't, however, I was not able to move forward in the direction I needed until I did. There are creative ways to get your board – trusted family, friends, community leaders with the same interest or even a

The Business Plan

board on demand that supports other organizations (Check out BlackCEO.com). An ideal board is not a multiple of people with titles. It just requires those willing to lend their time and knowledge to be a part of growing something greater than themselves creating change in this crazy world we live in. Yes, you do want to ensure that positions filled on your board matches skill sets and knowledge for future success.

You don't want to put someone in the position based on personal feelings or association. This is where courage is needed even if you choose the wrong person. Guess, what? Your Board is comprised of people with temporary and not a lifelong membership. If the person ultimately is a bad fit, don't be afraid to remove them or re-assess their skill sets – there might be another area that they might fit best within your business or personal goals.

However, trust will be the main key whichever structure you decide from all parties. If you have a board…I want to congratulate you. Now use them. They are your board to provide expertise advice to grow your company. Don't be afraid to ask your board the hard questions – *"why not?"* They will not be afraid to ask you hard questions so why not you. You do not have to do everything yourself, you do not have to have the solutions yourself – your board can help you. Valuing your board instills trust.

Look, my expertise is not in financials so I trust the CFO (Chief Financial Officer) to help in the decisions that impacts the organization and to keep the business growing – reach the community, to reach the nations – and keep us out of financial trouble. I don't know about you. I do not want to lose everything I have put my mind, soul and strength into. God says its mine and I am to prosper and those who help are to prosper too. However, I shouldn't be so foolish to not seek outside help. They are sowing seeds for their greater and you should be willing to give them the opportunity. Remember, "Iron sharpens

The Business Plan

Iron". The board can help you do just that. Whatever your goals are the board is there to help you achieve them and much more. Remember to use wisdom which is on your side. Just like you wouldn't purchase a car without details nor should you just take your boards advice. Take all things into consideration. Weigh the cost and seek wisdom in your final decision.

And it is okay if some outgrow your vision. Yes, just let them go. Remember some are just for a season and when the season has ended – *let them go*. New fruit will blossom with new ideas to take your vision further. Not to mention you will stop their growth by hanging on to them.

A must: Have a Board of Directors. You don't have to have a large board at first. Recommend at a minimum a Chief Financial Officer (CFO), Chief Legal Officer (CLO), Chief Sales Officer (CSO), and a COO (Chief Operations Officer).

The Business Plan

You can add a Chief Marketing Officer (CMO), Chief Social Media Officer (CSMO), and Chief Technology Officer (CTO) just to name a few as your business grows.

I pray that you discovered something new about yourself as you read this book. You will not have the answer to everything you will face in your journey. But know that you are not alone. Have faith and endure the process – there are many surprises along the way – some good and some not so good. Don't grow weary and remain focused on what God has designed and planned just for you.

I pray God's blessings and favor on your Legacy Journey.

Glossary

Gap Analysis – comparison of data to ensure best use of resources to move the organization toward its goals.

High-level growth – a breakdown of the organizations goals and strategies into subcategories (i.e. marketing, funding).

Resiliency – the capacity to recover quickly from difficult times.

SWOT Analysis – is a method that evaluates four areas of a business (strengths, weaknesses, opportunities, and threats) to help in achieving the organizations goals and objectives.

Tangible – physical assets (i.e. furniture, land, cash, stocks or bonds).

References

Dictionary.com - http://www.dictionary.com/

Goodreads - https://www.goodreads.com/author/quotes/88114.Myles_Munroe

Investopedia - https://www.investopedia.com/terms/g/gap-analysis.asp

Small Business Administration - https://www.sba.gov/business-guide/plan/write-your-business-plan-template#section-header-2

Sources

Unless otherwise annotated, scripture quotations are from the Holy Bible, English Standard Version. All rights reserved.

About the Author

Ms. Lia Abney's passion is teaching and sharing knowledge specifically to teens (7th – 12th Grade). She is the founder of Victory Leadership Group, Inc. a 501c3 nonprofit organization that offers workshops that prepare teens for success as they transition from high school into the workforce. She also offers workshops designed and tailored for adults and small businesses. Her motto is Building People – Building Kingdoms.

Lia is a 2008 graduate from University of Phoenix with a Masters in Management and Public Administration and is currently pursuing her doctorate with Walden University in Public Policy and Administration with emphasis in Leadership. Ms. Abney is also a consultant, motivational speaker and a published author.

She is the mother to three children (DeJuan, Tyler, and Chontele). Mother-in-Law to Haley (married to son DeJuan) and Grandmother to Makenzie. Ms. Abney currently resides in Hephzibah, Ga.

The Business Plan

Leave a review on Amazon.com

Book Lia Abney for your next event at

info@liaabneyllc.com

Now offering a 3 month goal setting session.
Individual and group sessions are available at
victoryleadershipgroupinc@gmail.com for
more details.

www.ingramcontent.com/pod-product-compliance
Lightning Source LLC
Chambersburg PA
CBHW030047230526
45471CB00003B/975